I0468964

Swear Word Coloring Book

RUDE CREATURES

SWEAR WORD COLORING BOOK FOR ADULTS

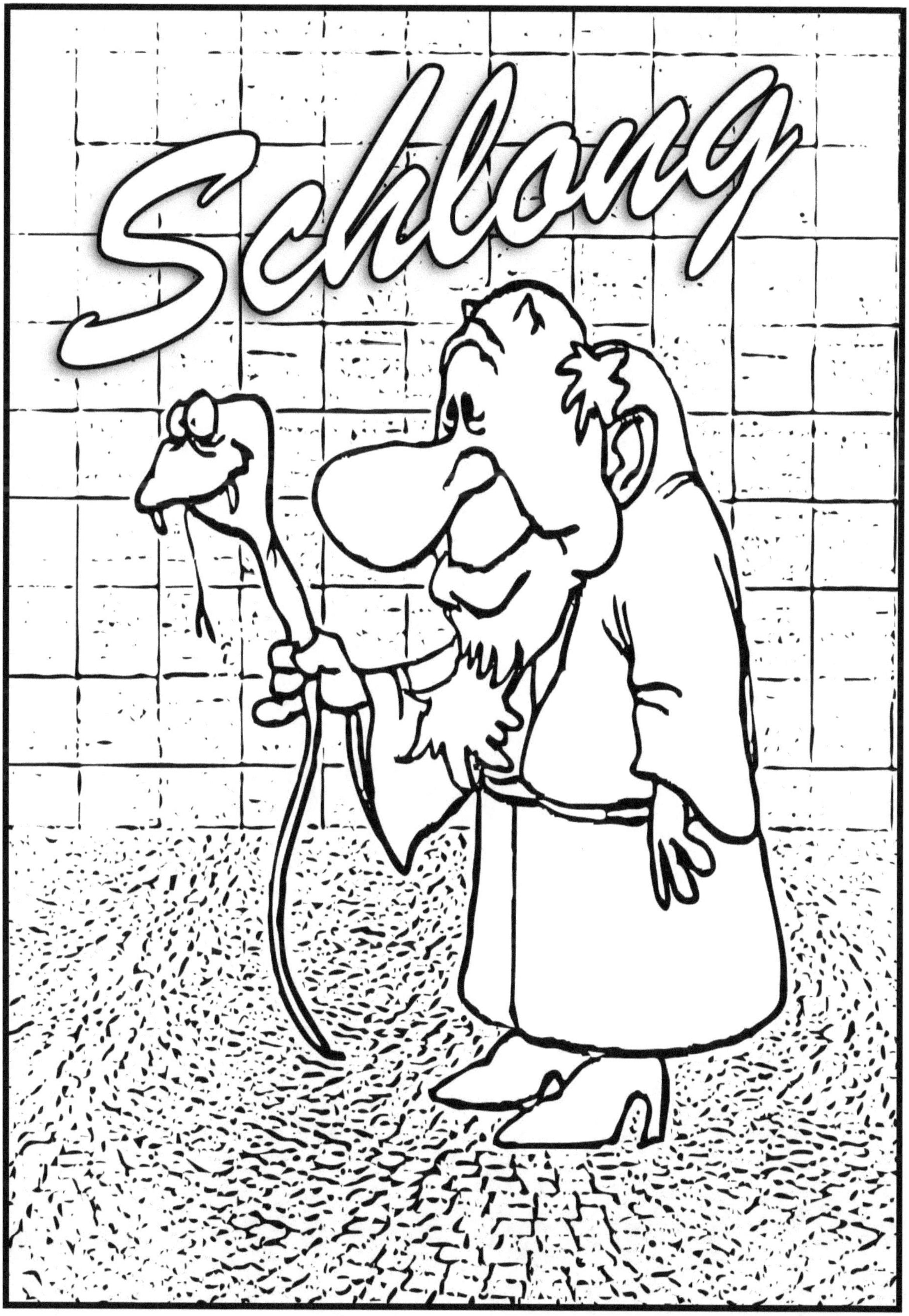
Schlong

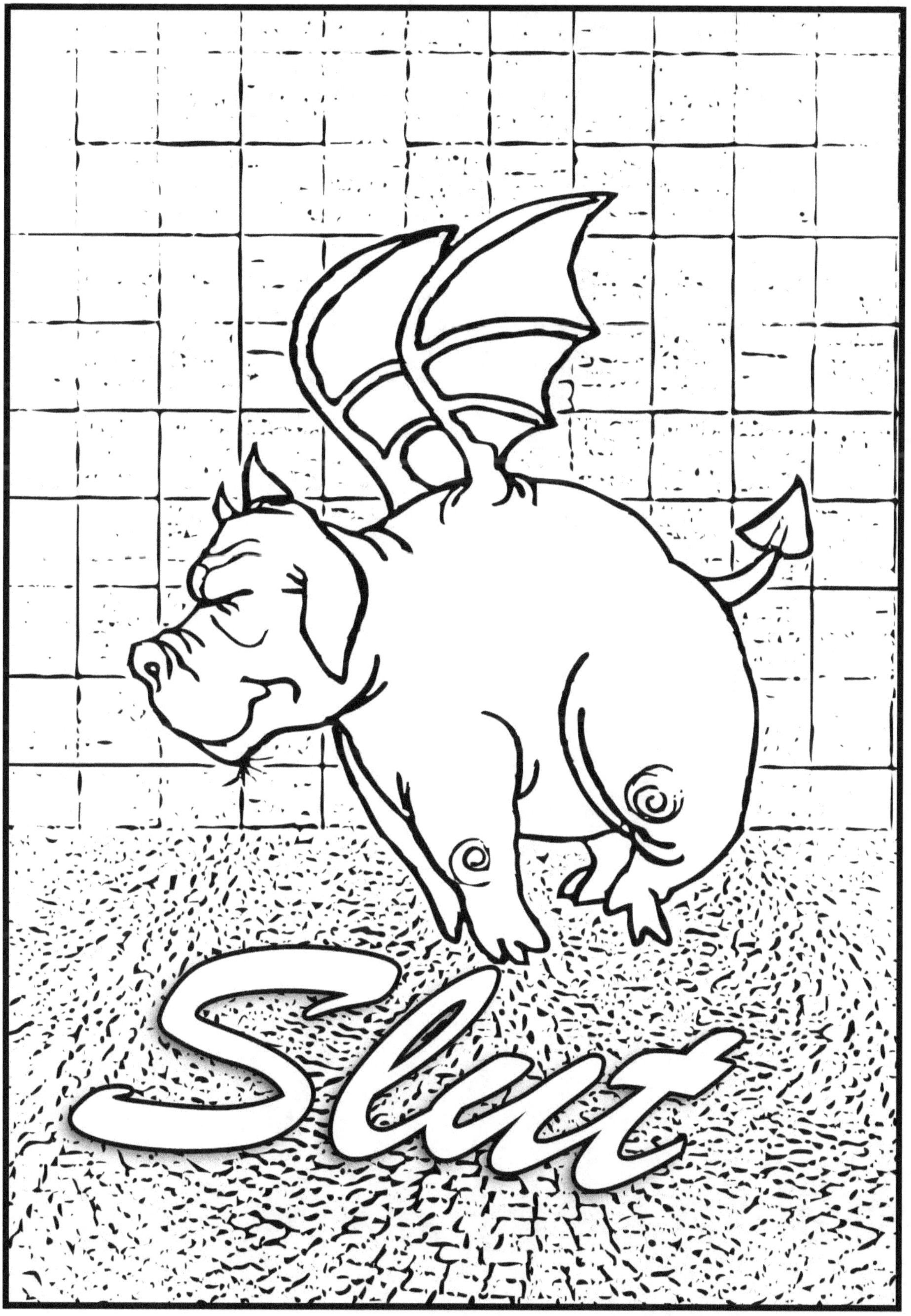
Slut

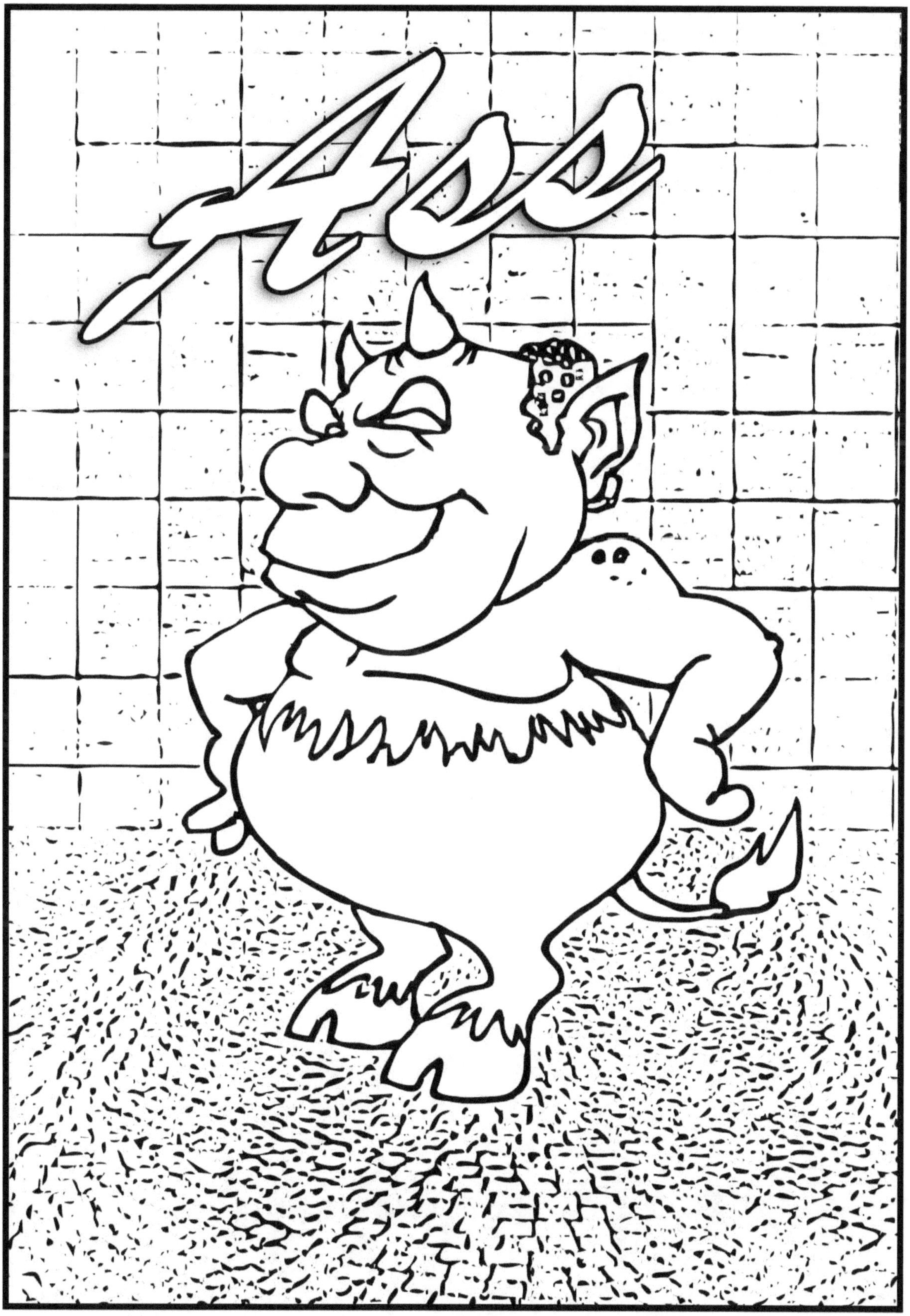
Ase

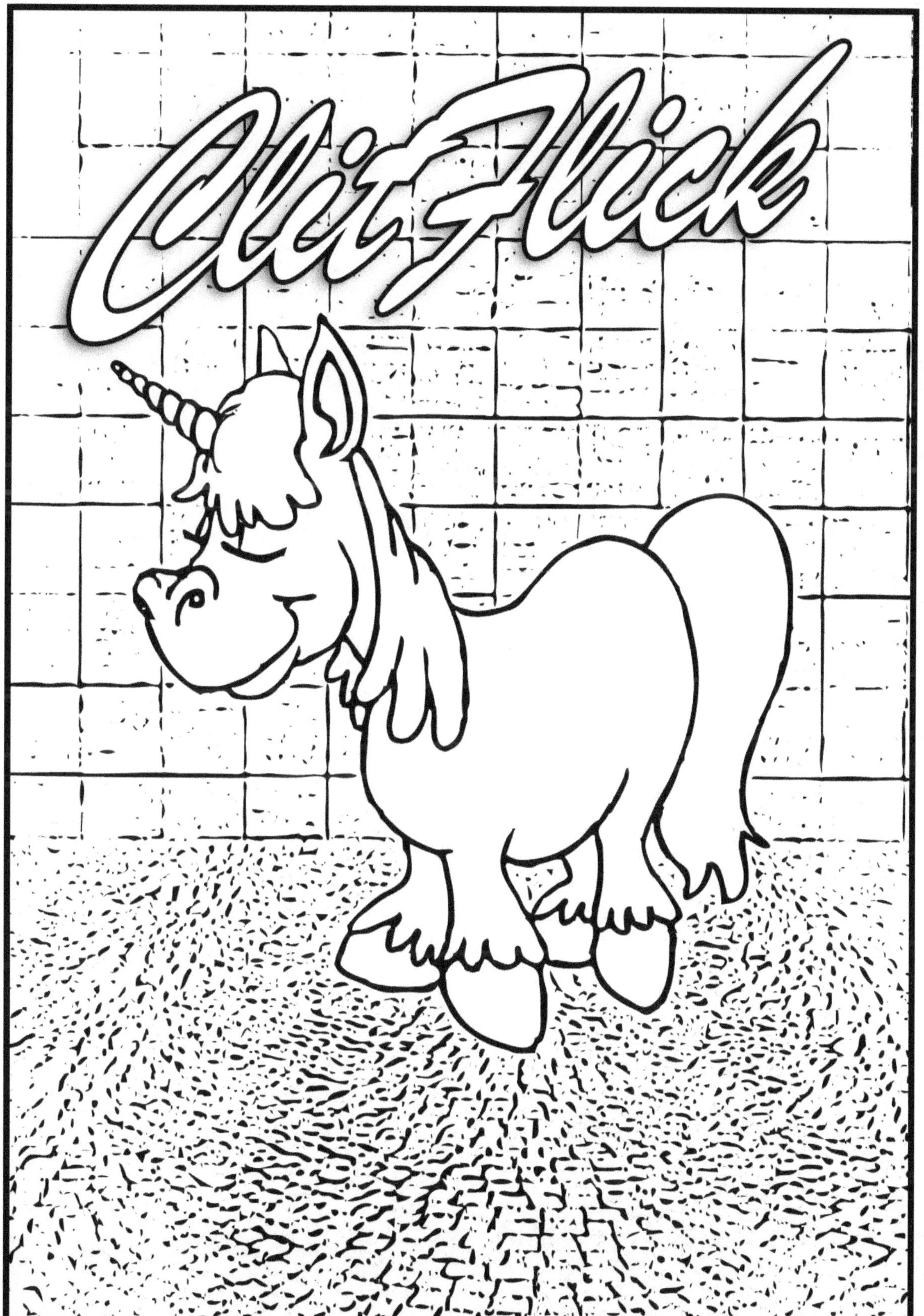
Clit Flick

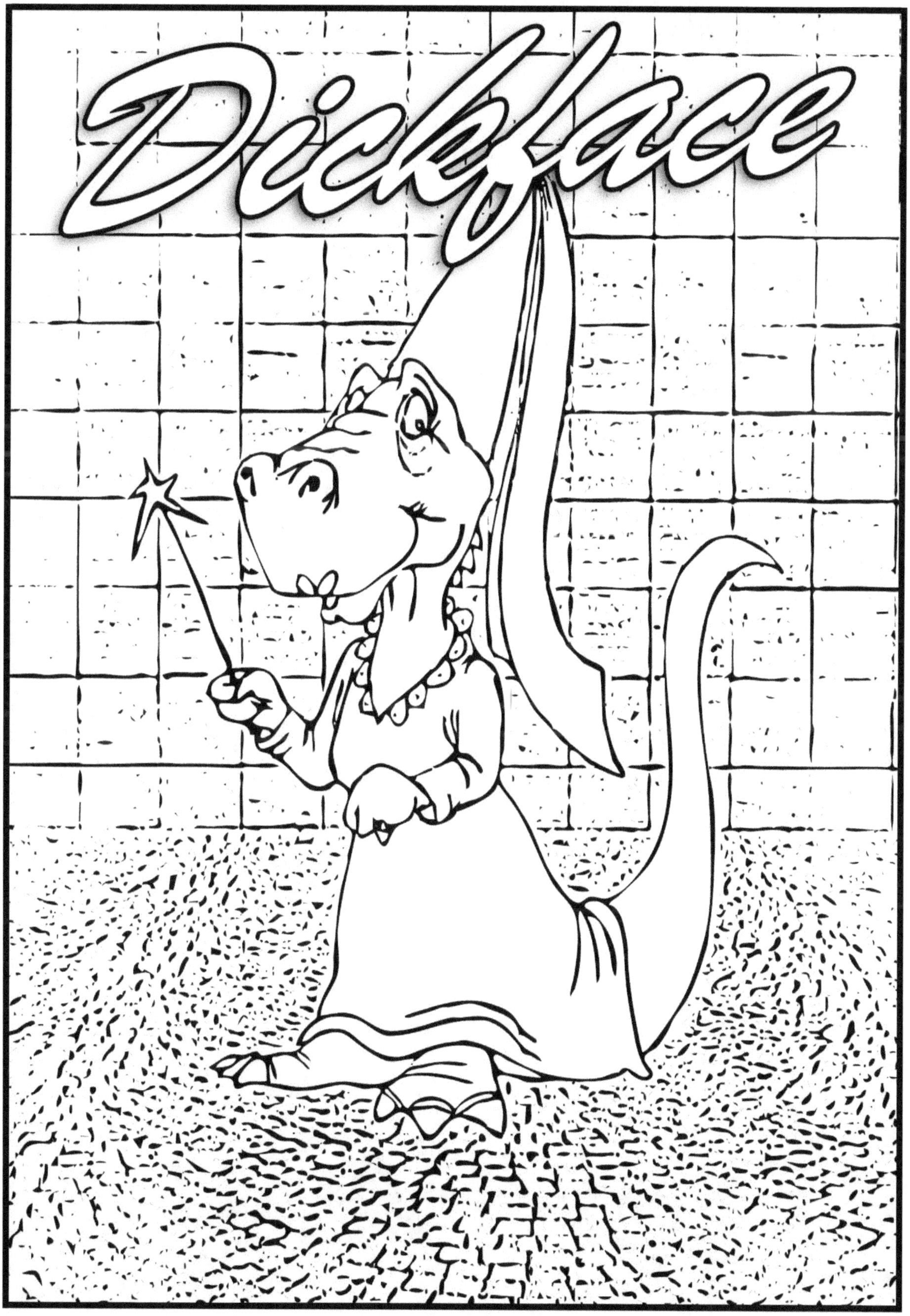
Dickface

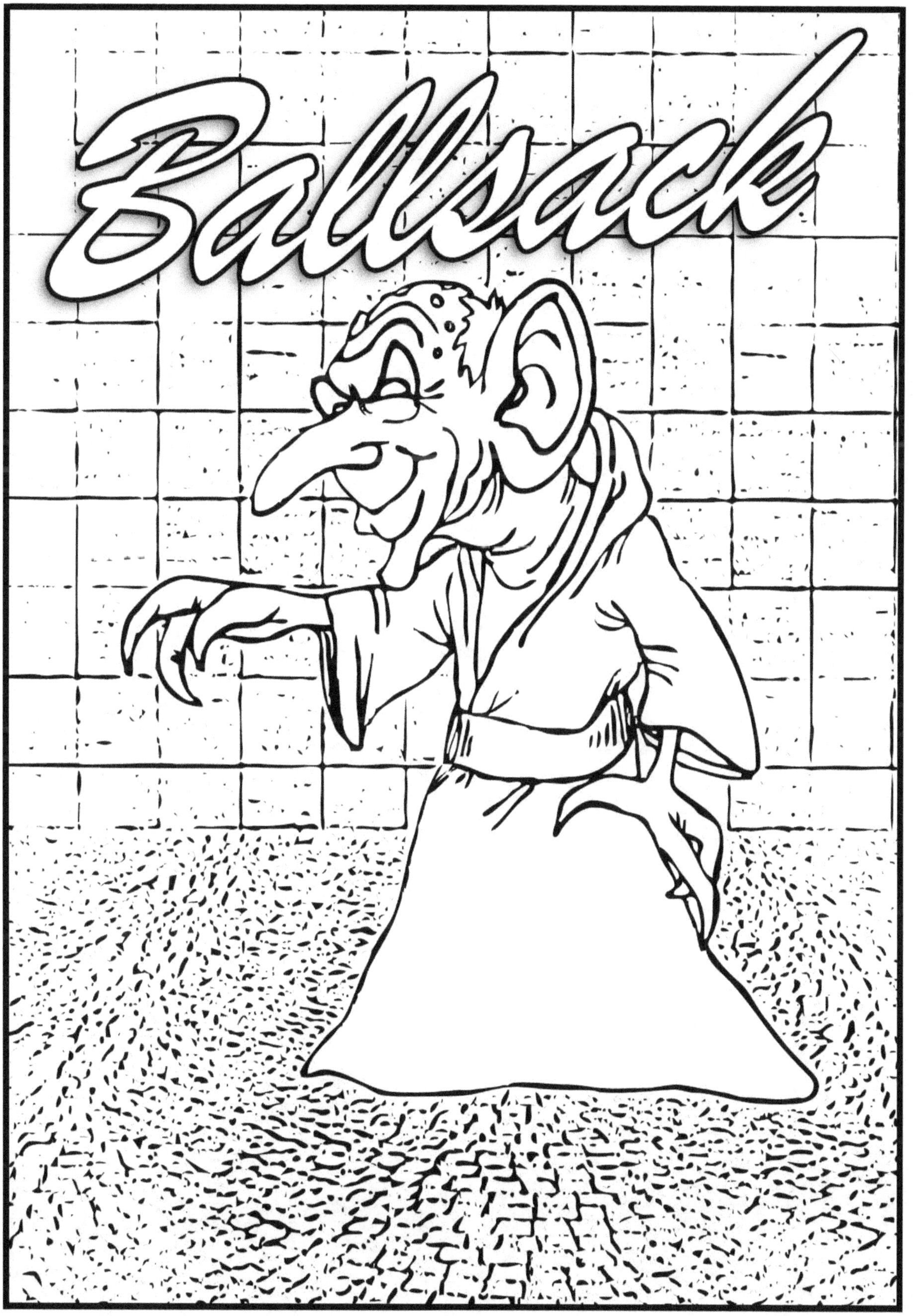
Ballsack

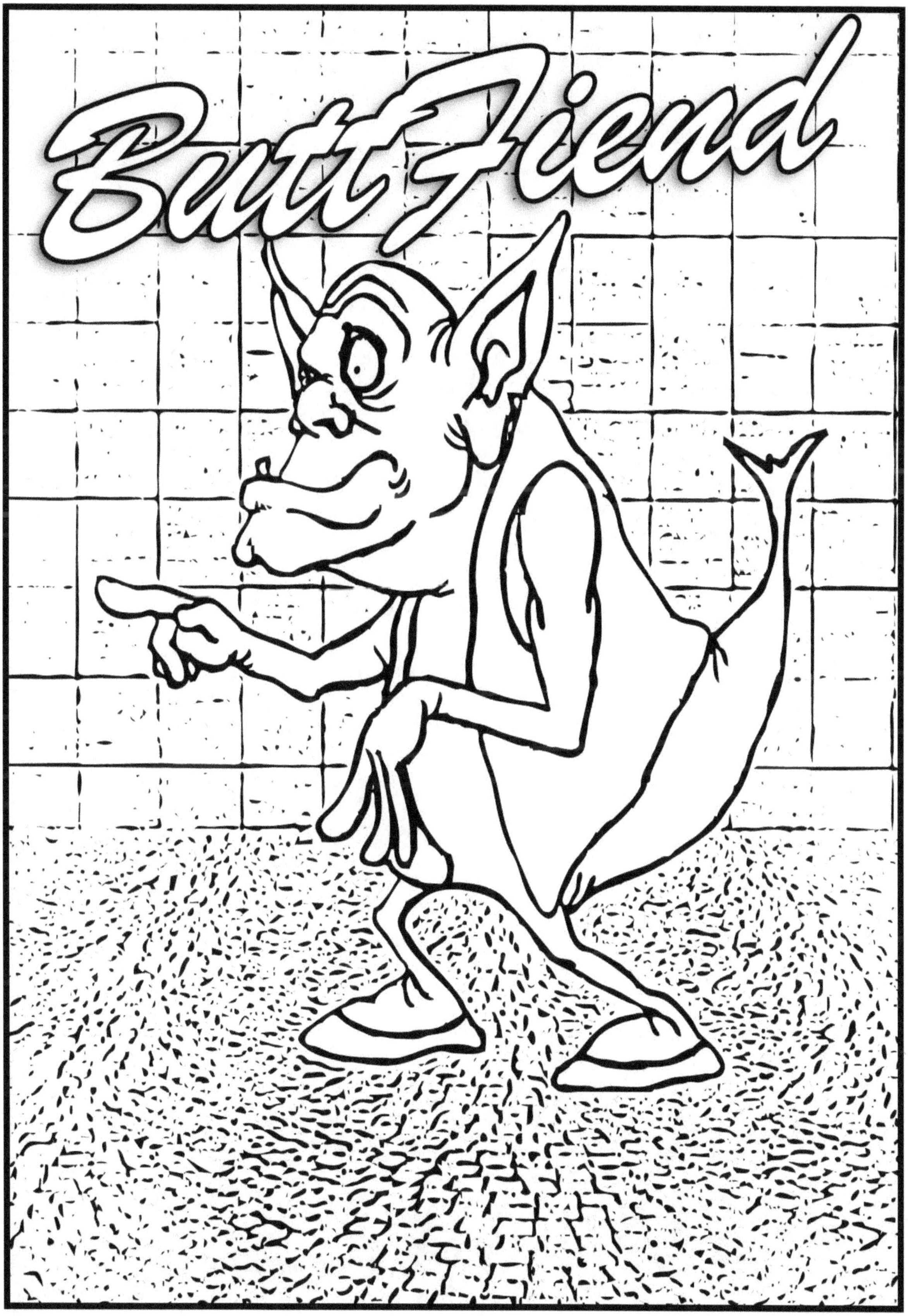
Butt Fiend

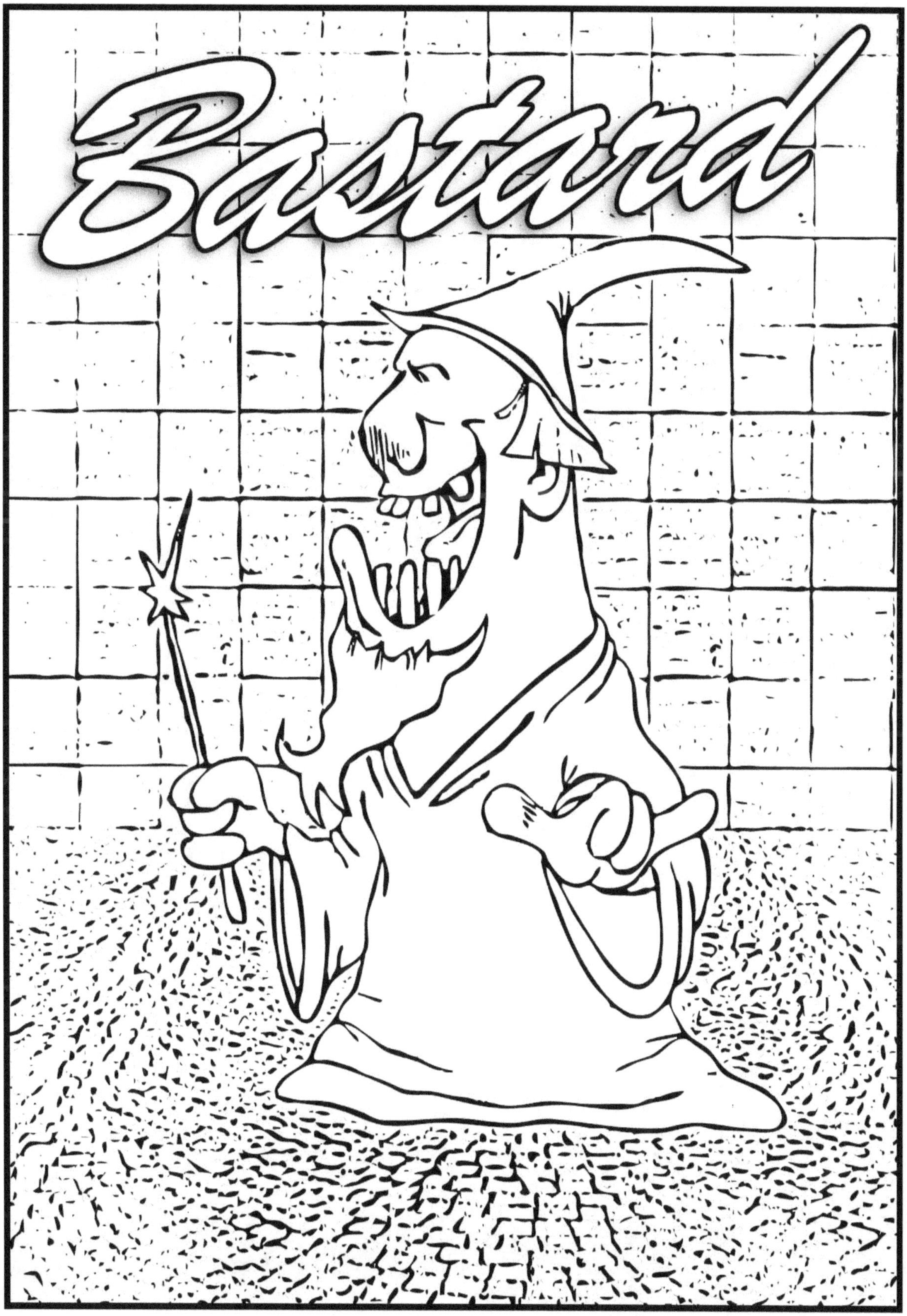
Bastard

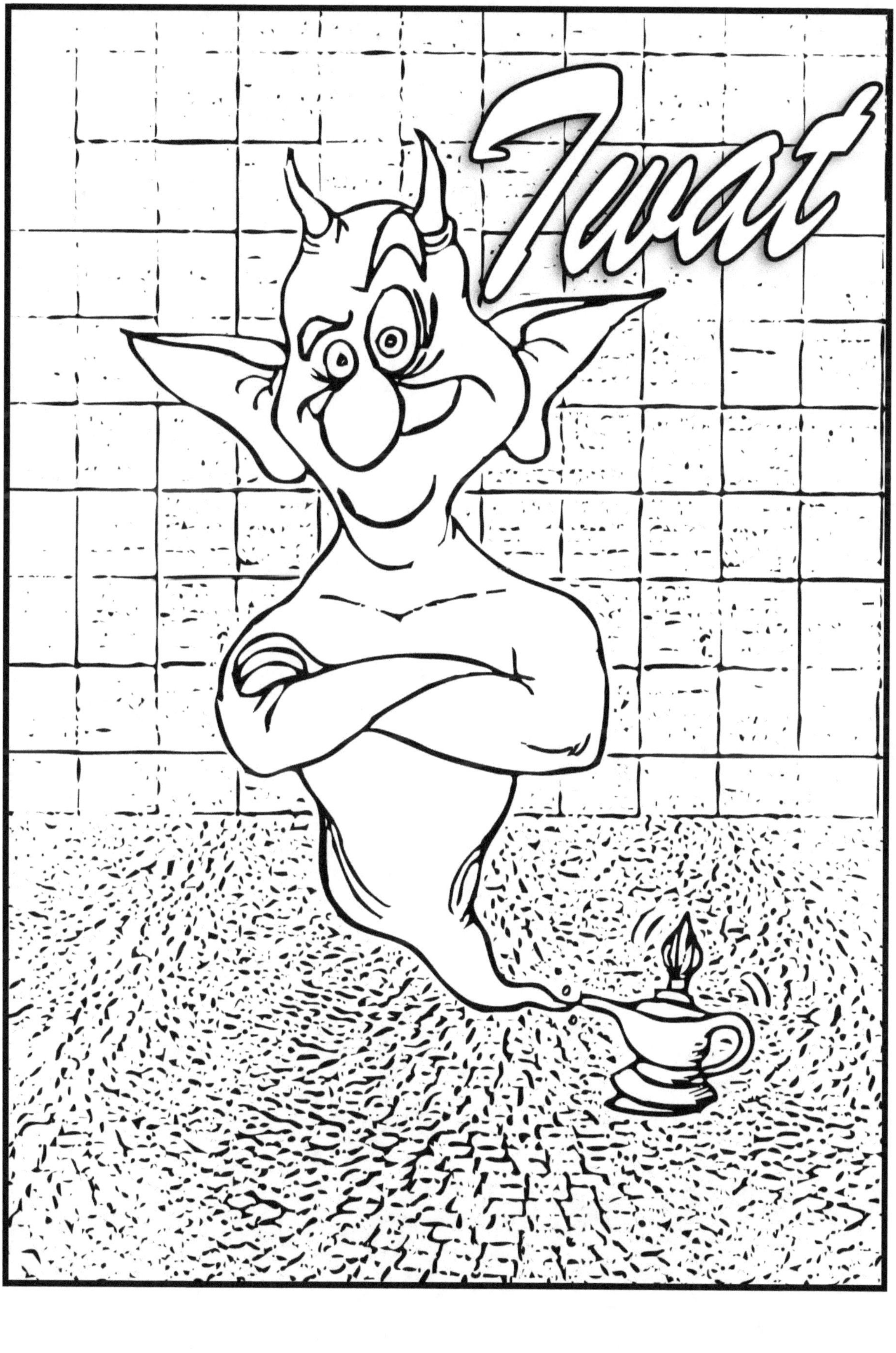
Twat

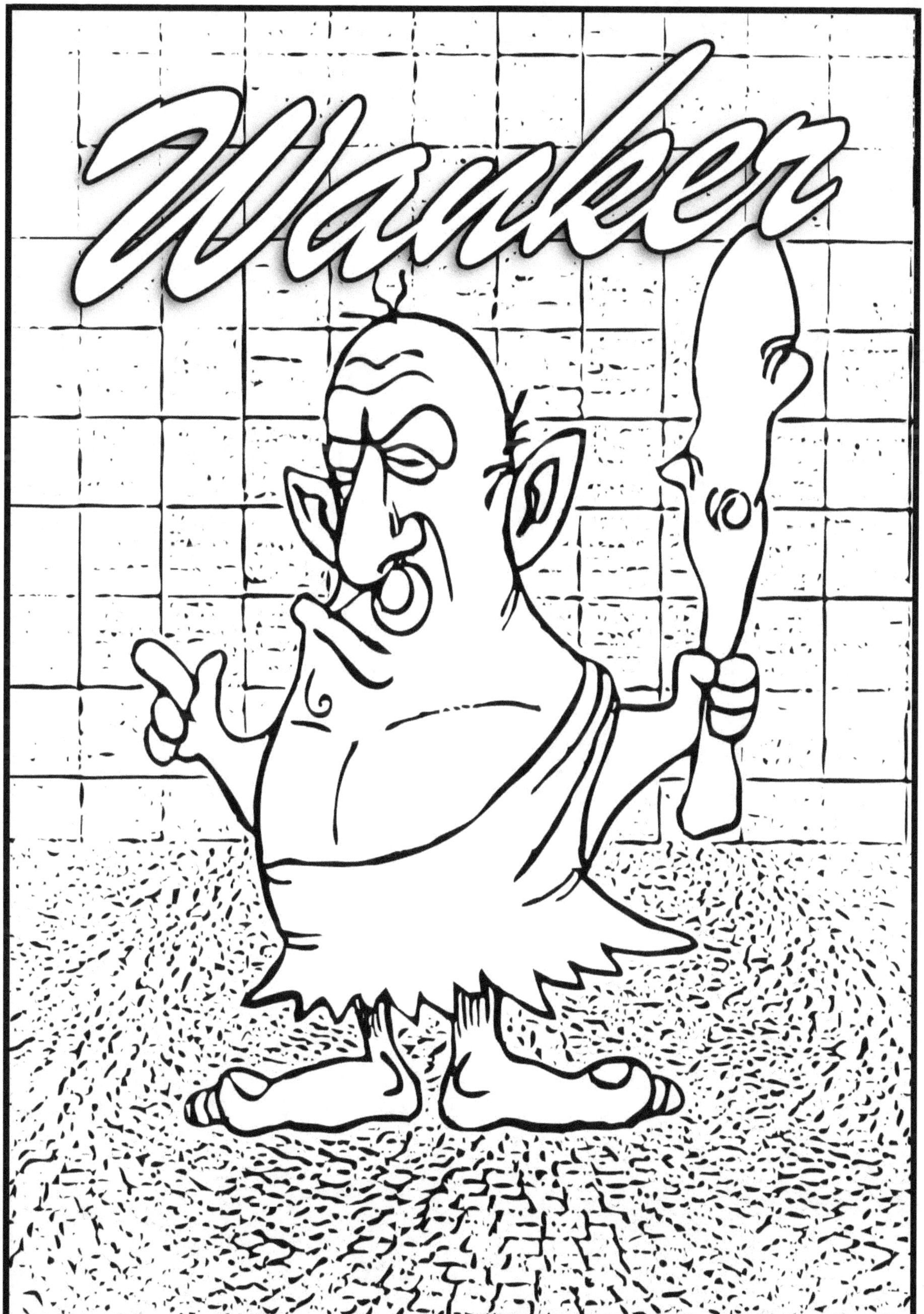
Wanker

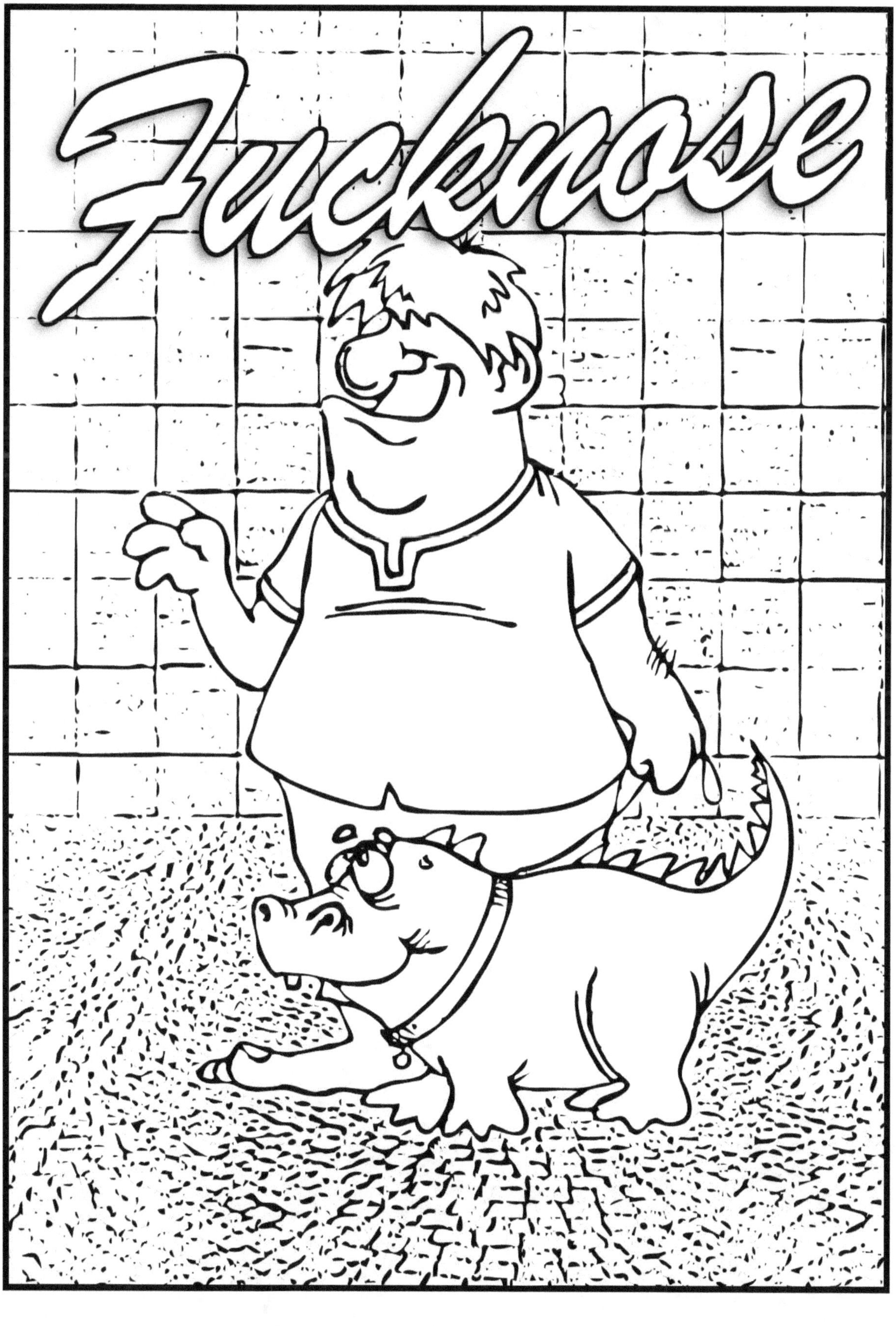
Fucknose

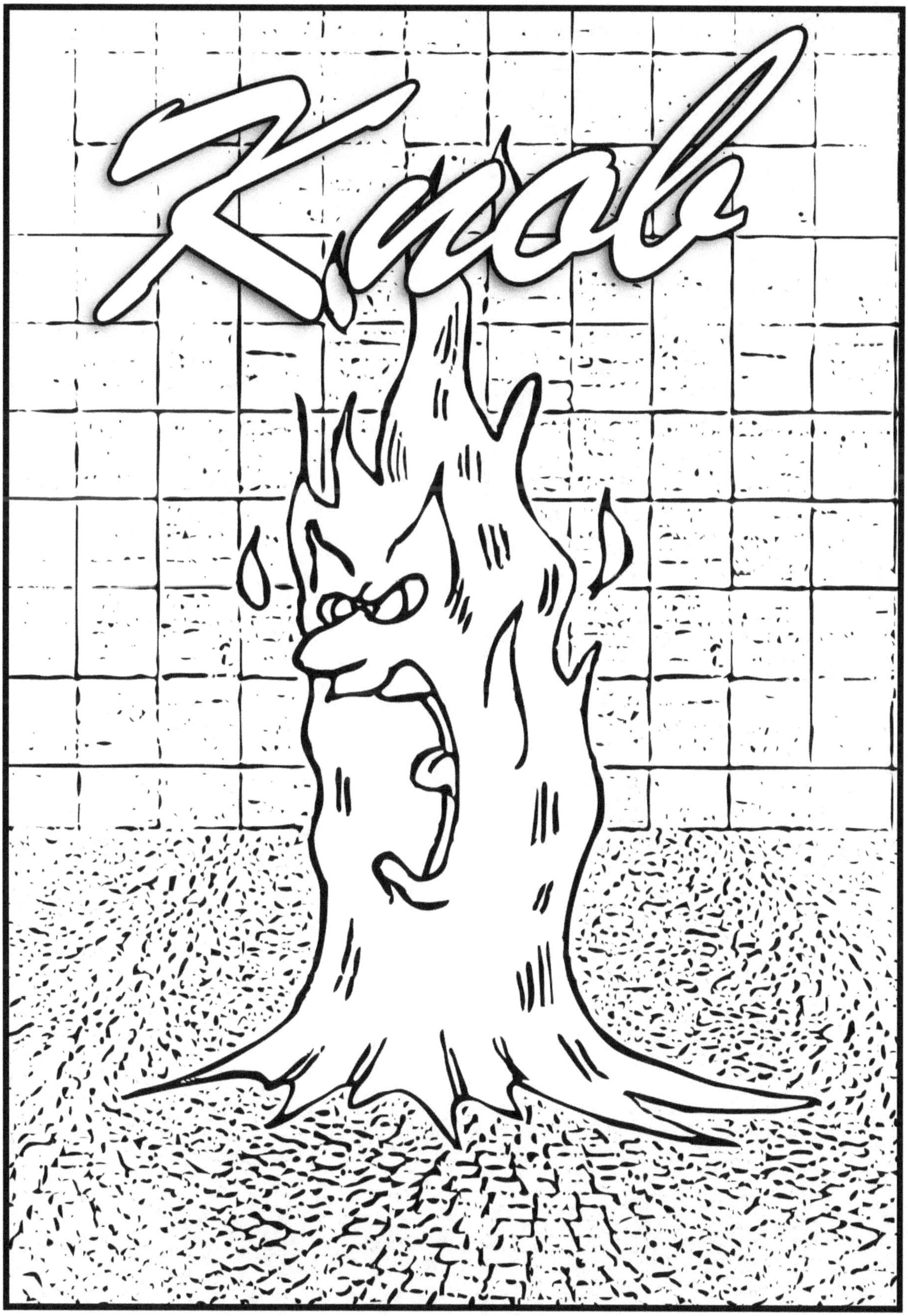
Knob

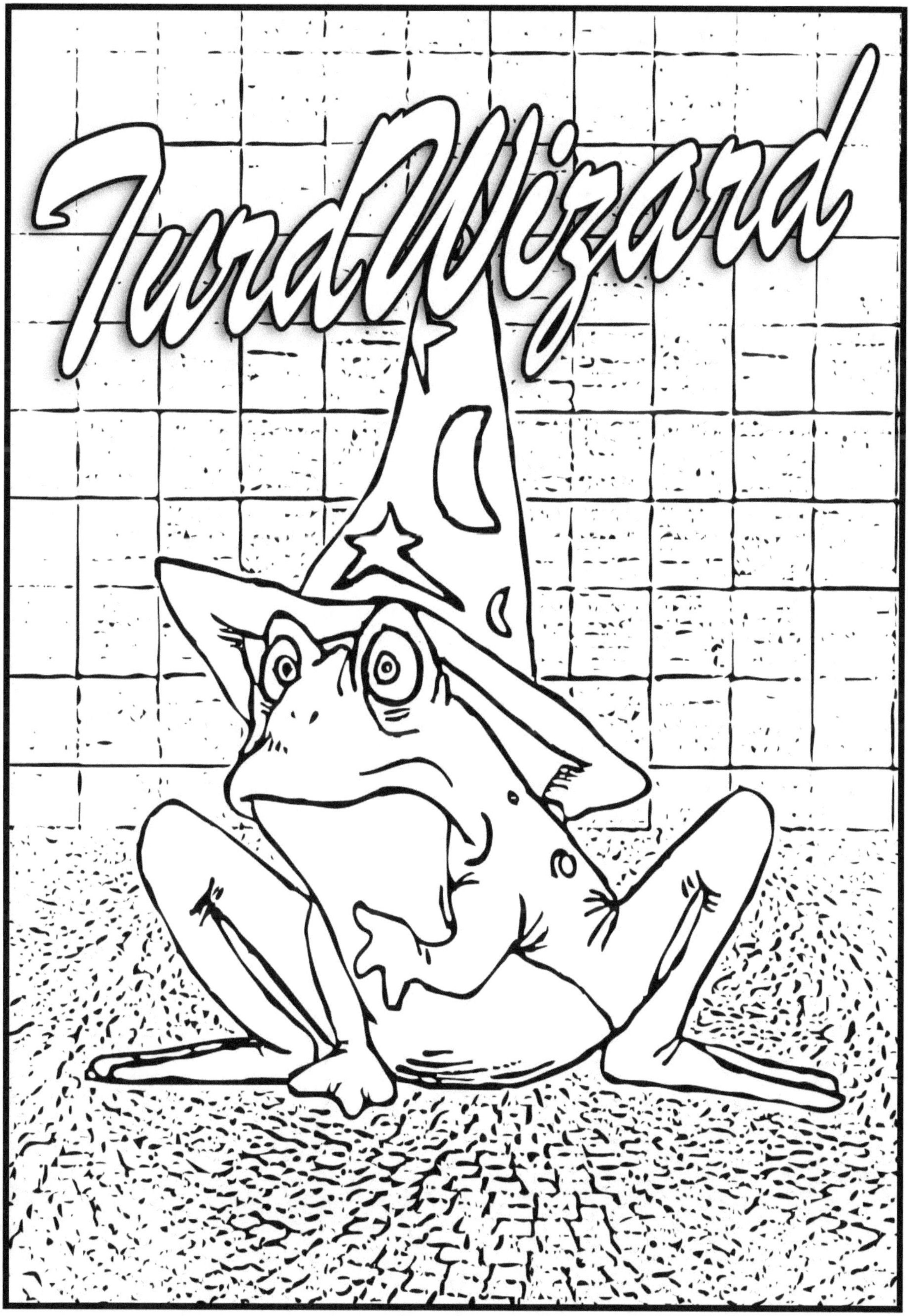

Turd Wizard

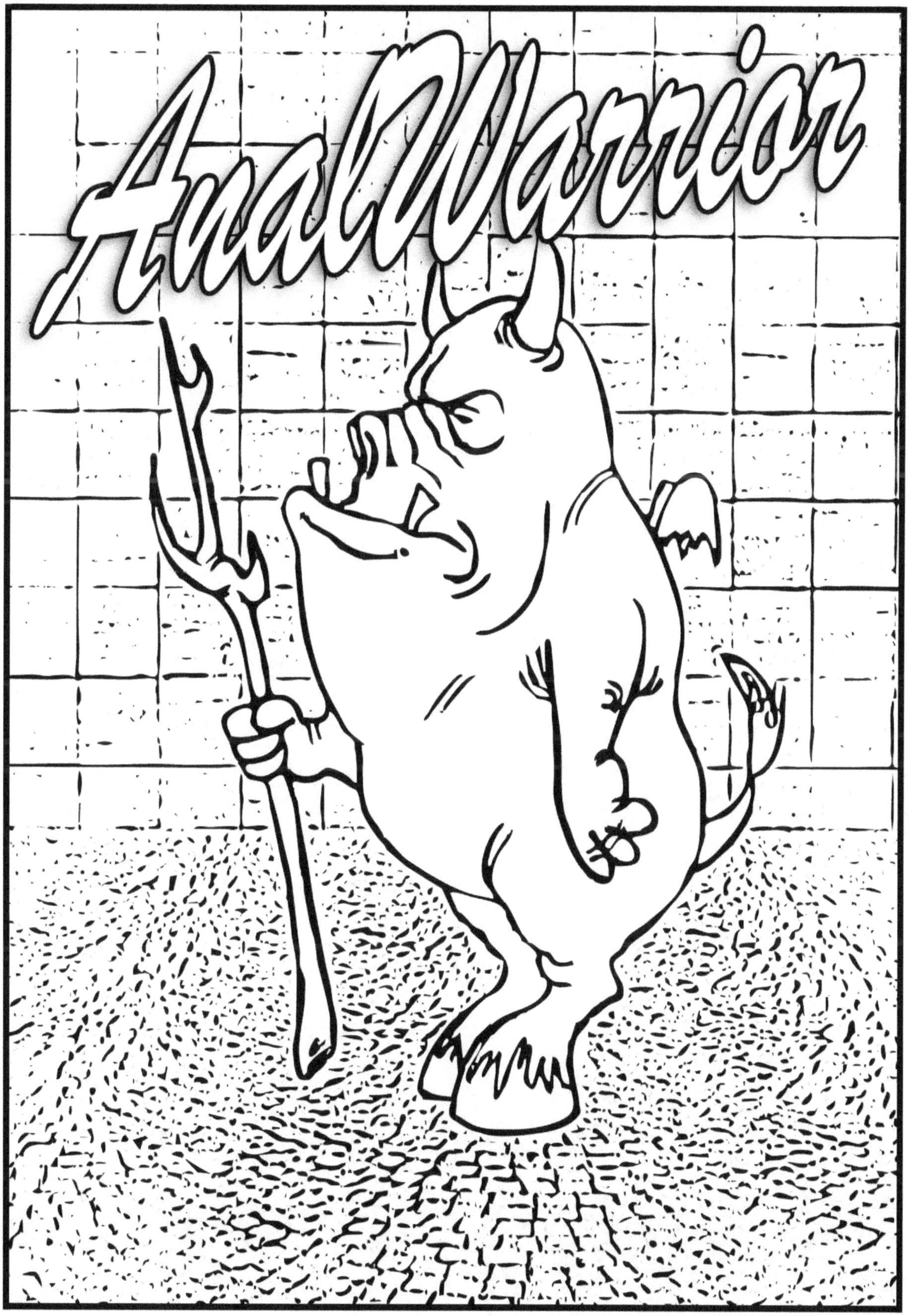
AnalWarrior

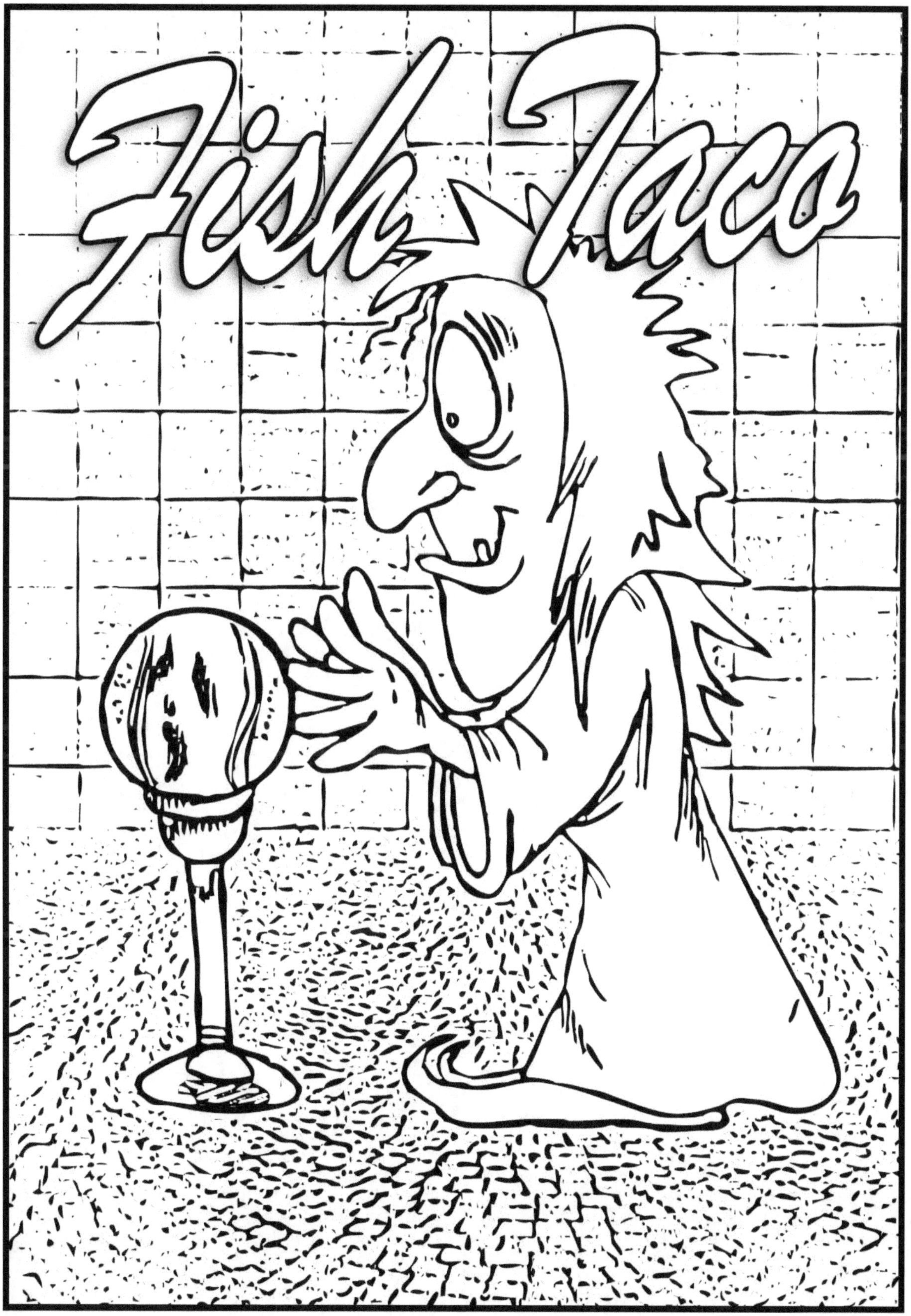
Fish Taco

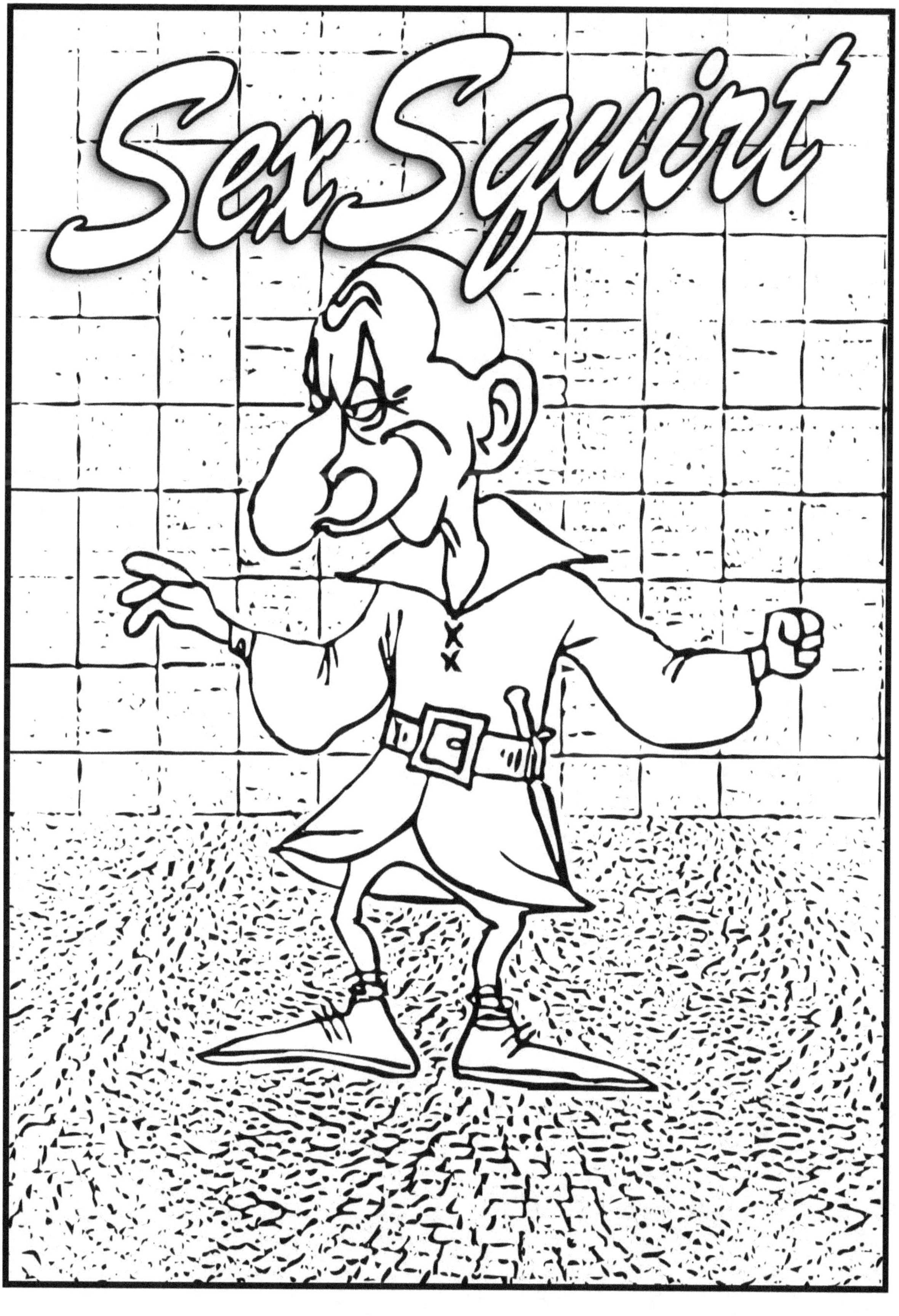
Sex Squirt

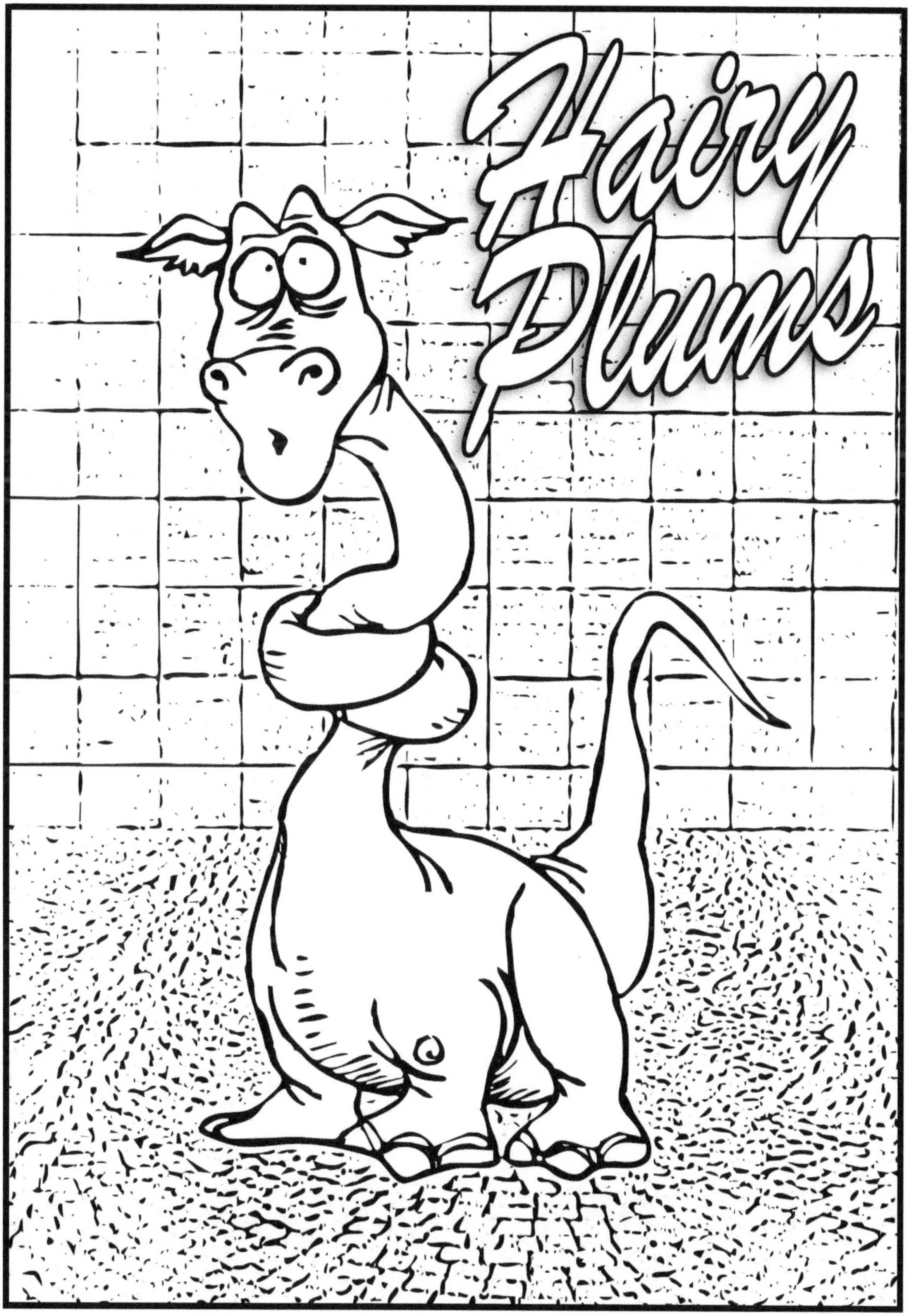
Hairy Plums

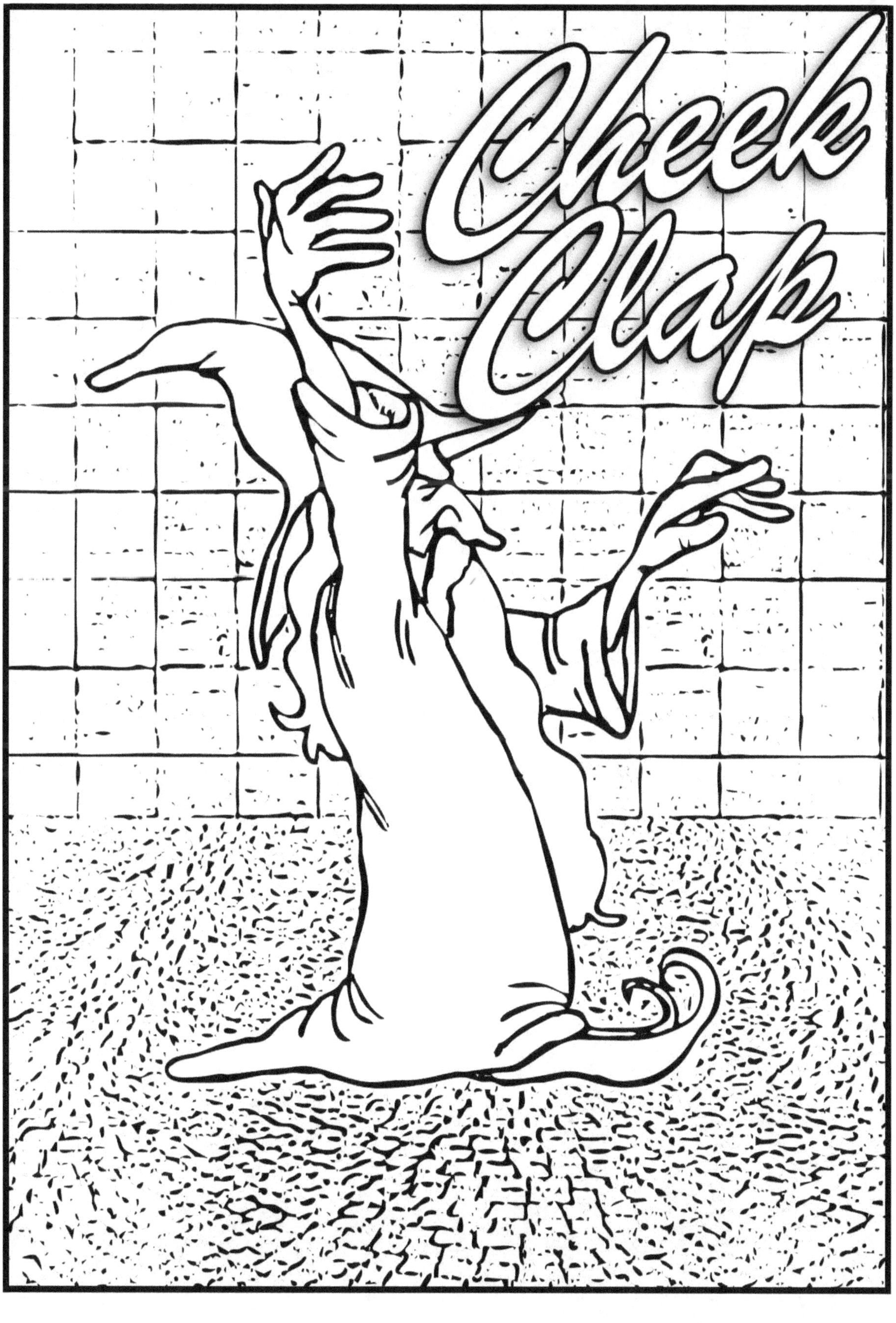
Cheek
Clap

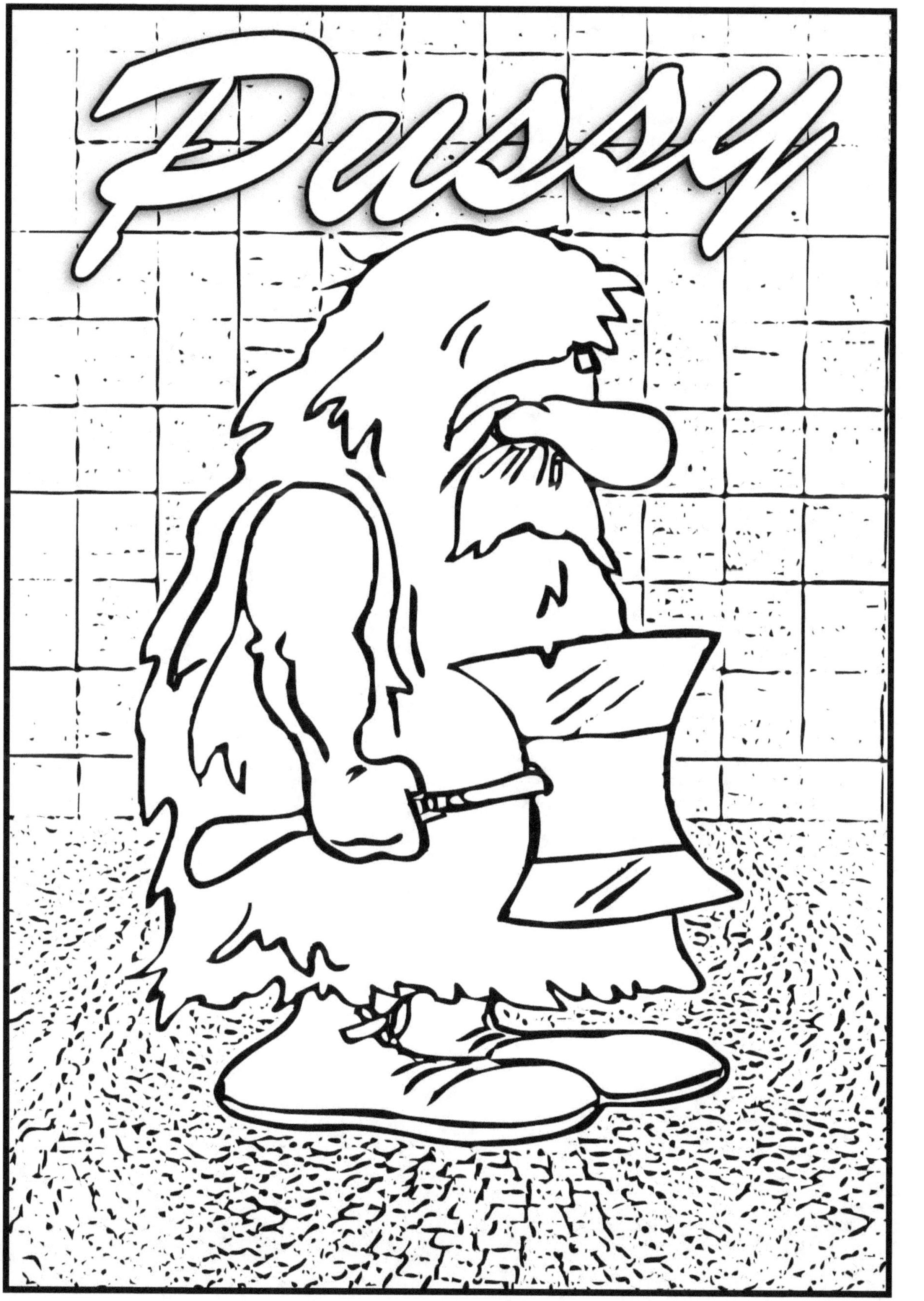
Pussy

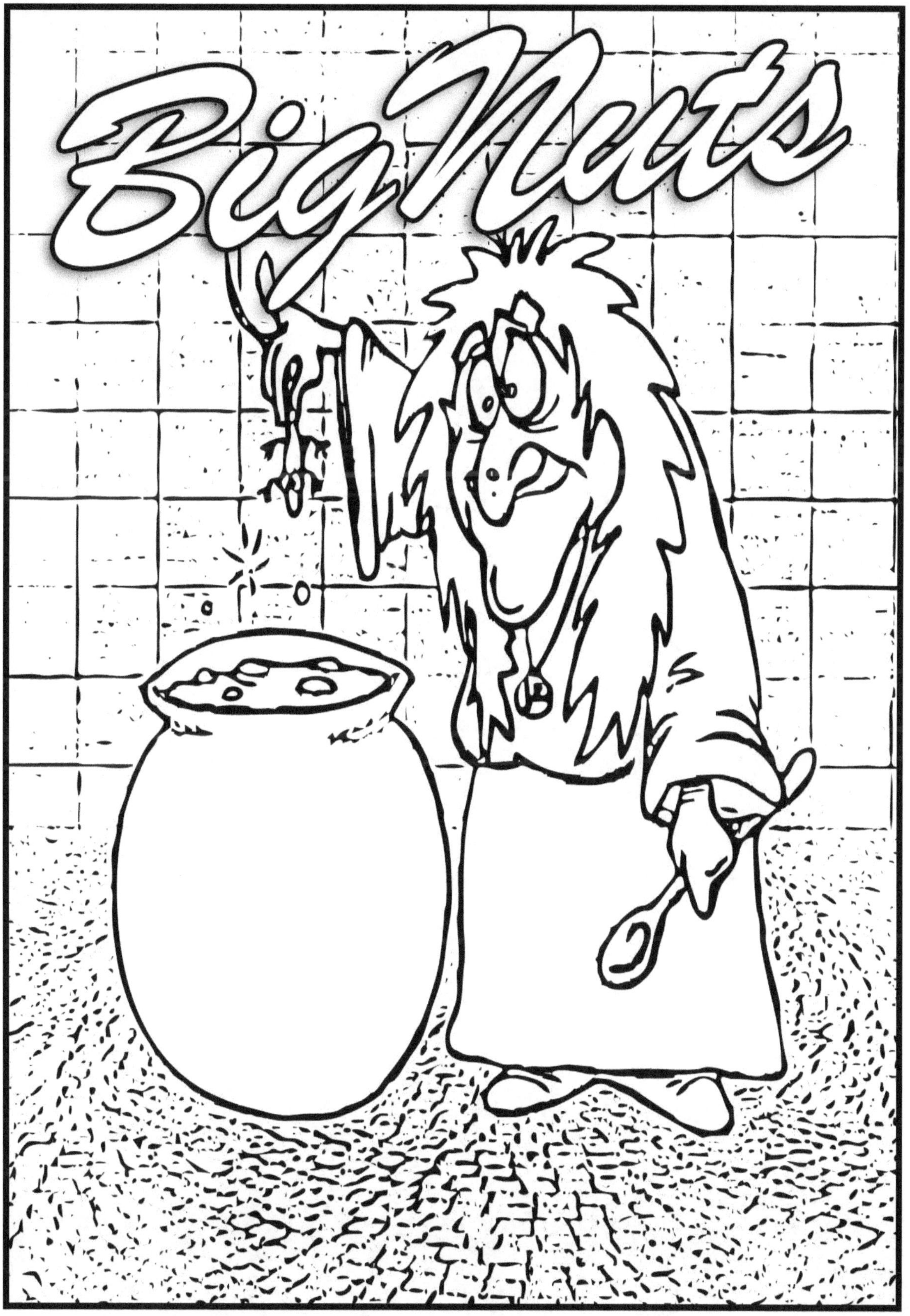
Big Nuts

www.ingramcontent.com/pod-product-compliance
Lightning Source LLC
Chambersburg PA
CBHW080612190526
45169CB00007B/2984
9781530034123